Contents

Introduction

Throughout history flowers have been depicted in many different ways. They have always been a popular subject: artists have captured their fresh beauty on canvas; textile workers have been inspired by their form and colour; and embroiderers have used them to transform their fabrics and canvasses, enriching designs with textures and colours.

I have had an avid love of flowers all my life. I live not a stone's throw away from where I was born, in a narrow village lane that winds its way through woodland down to a river. The hedgerows, woodland glades and the riverbank have always abounded with wild flowers, and the delight of seeing these flowers today is the same as it was when I was a child. One way or another, flowers seem to touch us all, and my particular love is to capture their colour and shape with silk ribbon embroidery.

Silk ribbon has a beautiful sheen and is available in a wide range of subtle shades, making it an ideal medium for recreating many different flowers. It is so soft and fine that it can be threaded on a needle and stitched exactly the same way as traditional embroidery threads. However, unlike thread, embroidered silk ribbon creates a three-dimensional effect which adds depth to any design.

__Opposite and above__

Although the projects in this book are designed to be framed and hung on the wall as pictures, silk ribbon embroidery is ideal for lots of other applications.

Use the single rose bud design shown on page 1 to create a stunning cushion cover. Decorate a picture frame for your favourite photograph, or add a touch of class to the lid of a pretty glass container. Silk ribbon can even be used to decorate jewellery. The enlarged detail of the necklace shows how to use a single rose to good effect.

Beginner's guide to
Silk Ribbon Embroidery

Ann Cox

SEARCH PRESS

First published in Great Britain 1998

Search Press Limited
Wellwood, North Farm Road,
Tunbridge Wells, Kent TN2 3DR

Reprinted 1999, 2000, 2001, 2002, 2004

Text copyright © Ann Cox 1998

Photographs by Search Press Studios
Photographs and design copyright © Search Press Ltd.
1998

ISBN 0 85532 835 5

Suppliers
If you have any difficulty in obtaining any of the materials and equipment mentioned in this book, then please write to the publishers for a current list of stockists, which includes firms who operate a mail-order service:

Search Press Limited, Wellwood,
North Farm Road, Tunbridge Wells,
Kent TN2 3DR, England

I would like to thank my husband, Ashley, for his constant support during the preparation of this book; for his endless patience with me and the computer (at times we became quite incompatible); and for his useful and tactful suggestions.

My thanks go also to my parents, Nora and Bill Wilson, for their encouragement and for their permission to use their wedding photograph; to Muriel Elliott, who was so often a sounding board for my ideas and was always constructive with her advice; and to all my students who initially inspired me to write this book and who, with their eager enthusiasm, have kept me on my toes ever since.

I would also like to thank Framecraft of 372–376 Summer Lane, Hockley, Birmingham, England for their kind help in supplying the trinket box and other containers featured on pages 5 and 7.

Metric/imperial measurements

Silk ribbons are only available in metric widths: 2, 4, 7 and 13mm. Approximate imperial sizes are $\frac{1}{16}$, $\frac{1}{8}$, $\frac{1}{4}$ and $\frac{1}{2}$in. Other linear measurements convert as follows:

5mm ($\frac{3}{16}$in)	12.5cm (5in)	40cm (16in)	2.5m (8ft)
1cm ($\frac{3}{8}$in)	18cm (7in)	0.5m (20in)	3m (10ft)
2.5cm (1in)	20cm (8in)	1m (40in)	4m (13ft)
6.5cm (2$\frac{1}{2}$in)	25cm (10in)	1.5m (5ft)	5m (16ft)
7.5cm (3in)	30cm (12in)	2m (6ft 6in)	

Publisher's note
All the step-by-step photographs in this book feature the author, Ann Cox, demonstrating how to embroider with silk ribbons. No models have been used.

Colour separation by P&W Graphics, Singapore
Printed in Malaysia by Times Offset (M) Sdn Bhd

Page 1
Ivory silk dupion is pin-tucked diagonally to form diamond shapes. The rosebuds are worked with 7mm ribbon, in three shades of pink. The dark centre petals are lazy daisy stitches, whilst ribbon stitch is used for those on either side and for the calyx.

Right
Different shades of pink 7mm ribbon are used with one-, two and three-loop French knots to form the clusters of flowers on this climbing rose.

In this book I show you how to use four basic stitches (ribbon stitch, which is unique to ribbon embroidery, straight stitch, French knot and lazy daisy stitch) and I also demonstrate a range of gathering techniques which I use to create a wide variety of flowers and plants.

Observe the flowers and plants around you or study pictures of them. Look at their general shape and colour; at their size relative to other plants; at the edge and curve of their petals and leaves; and at how all the different elements of the plants are connected by stems.

When you really start to compare different flowers, you will soon discover how similar some of them are, but also what makes them identifiable and unique. For example, by changing the colour and width of the ribbon, and the number and/or position of the stitches, you can change a marigold into an aster or even a wallflower, a rose into a peony, or a towering delphinium into a delicate spray of gypsophila.

You do not have to be artistic, or to have any special skills to embroider flowers with silk ribbons. Once you have learned the basic stitches, you will be ready to work through the projects. To help guide you through each project, I have included a basic template for each design and step-by-step illustrations. There are over sixty flowers illustrated in this book, and I am sure that you will soon be designing your own arrangements.

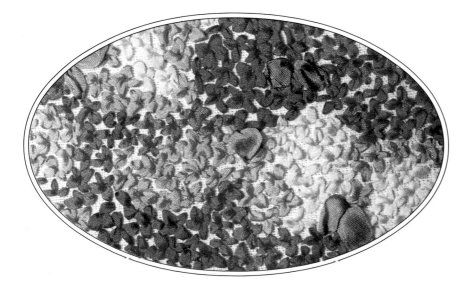

Opposite and left

A few more examples of how you can use your silk ribbon embroidery.

The picture was inspired by pots on my own patio, and embroidered with a great deal of imagination – the flowers in the real pots have never grown with such profusion. All four stitches described on the following pages are used to recreate the blooms.

In contrast, the mophead hydrangeas on the cushion (shown full-size in the detail left), are made using just straight stitch (see page 17). Ribbon stitch (see page 15) is used to form the green leaves.

The gathering technique (see pages 21 and 38) is used to create the cluster of wild poppies that contrasts beautifully with the rich, dark wood of the trinket box.

Calico

Silk noile

Silk dupion

Linen/cotton
evenweave

Surface linen

Tools and materials

The essential tools and materials comprise the silk ribbon itself, some backing fabric, a few needles, a pair of scissors and an embroidery hoop. These are all readily available at needlecraft suppliers, but you may have to go to the larger outlets to find a full range of ribbon widths and colours. I have also included details of other tools and materials that you may want to add to your workbox.

Ribbons

Pure silk ribbon is available in a wonderful range of colours, and in four different widths: 2, 4, 7 and 13mm. It differs from other types of ribbon in that it is very soft; it can therefore be used in exactly the same way as a thread, and embroidered through the fabric using traditional stitches.

However, in keeping with other forms of fine silk, the ribbon can snag. It should therefore always be handled and stored very carefully.

Fabrics

You can embroider on to any fabric that allows a needle to pass through it. Silk is a natural fibre and, to me, the ribbons are most compatible with other natural fibre fabrics such as wool, cotton or linen.

In the picture opposite I show you some of the fabrics that I like to use for my embroideries. The full-size insets featuring embroidered silk ribbon roses show you the different textures these fabrics possess. All are readily available and are pleasing to work with.

Opposite
Some of my favourite fabrics: calico, silk noile, silk dupion, surface linen and linen/cotton evenweave.

Needles

Use only chenille and crewel needles for the projects in this book. Chenille needles, with their sharp points and large eyes, are perfect for use with ribbons – use a medium size (No. 24) for 2mm ribbon and a large size (No. 18) for the wider ribbon. Use a fine crewel needle (No. 8) for embroidering other threads.

Threads

You will need a selection of stranded embroidery threads to anchor your ribbons to the fabric. These threads are also used for the running stitches in gathered flowers (see page 21). The stitches will usually be hidden from sight on the finished piece but it is better to match their colour to that of the ribbon.

I also use coton à broder and pearl cotton for items such as flower stems.

Other items

To complete the projects you will also need a pencil, a tape measure and some tracing paper to prepare the patterns; a small pair of sharp, pointed scissors to cut the ribbon and to trim off excess thread; an embroidery hoop and cotton binding strips or an adjustable frame and silk pins to work the embroidery on; and some dressmaker's pins to attach the template.

Some of the projects have stencilled and painted backgrounds. For these you will need a selection of stencil paints, fabric paints, brushes, and a tile or saucer to use as a palette.

Right

1. Stencil paintbrush
2. Stencil paints
3. Silk ribbons
4. Embroidery frames
5. Fabric paints
6. Tile palette
7. Scissors
8. Needles
9. Fabric
10. Dressmaker's pins
11. Paint brushes
12. Tape measure
13. Pencil
14. Embroidery threads
15. Silk pins

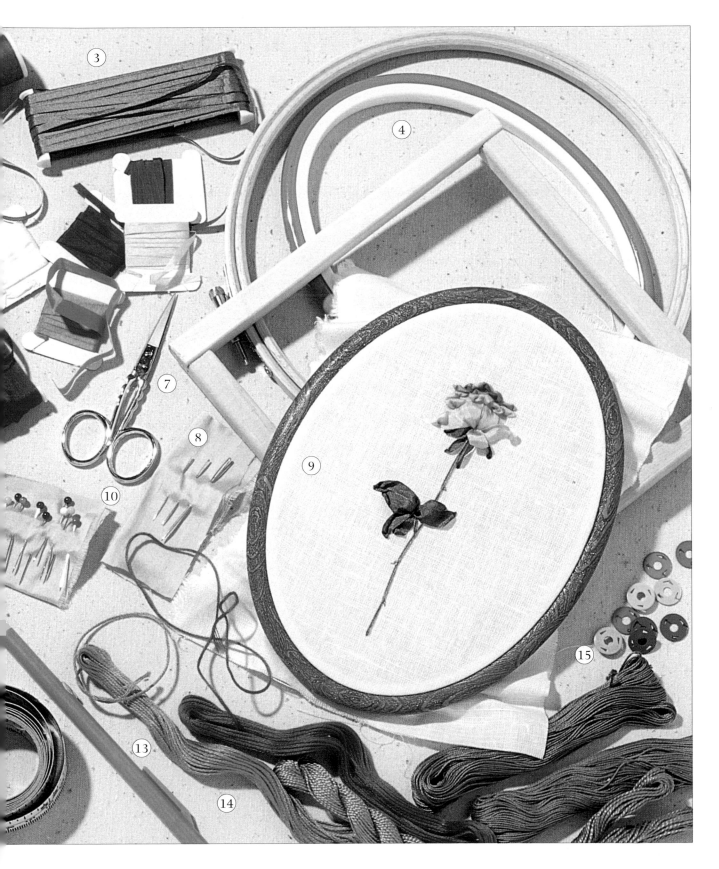

Embroidering with silk ribbons

Silk ribbon is a delight to work with. Each ribbon stitch covers more fabric than traditional thread, so designs take shape very quickly. Silk ribbon also adds a three-dimensional effect to an image. You can vary the size of each stitch by using different widths of ribbon, by changing the tension applied and by the size of the stitch.

However, silk ribbon does deteriorate each time it passes through the fabric, so always work with a relatively short length – 30cm or less is ideal.

Use a small pair of sharp scissors to cut each end of a length of ribbon at an angle of 45° to prevent fraying.

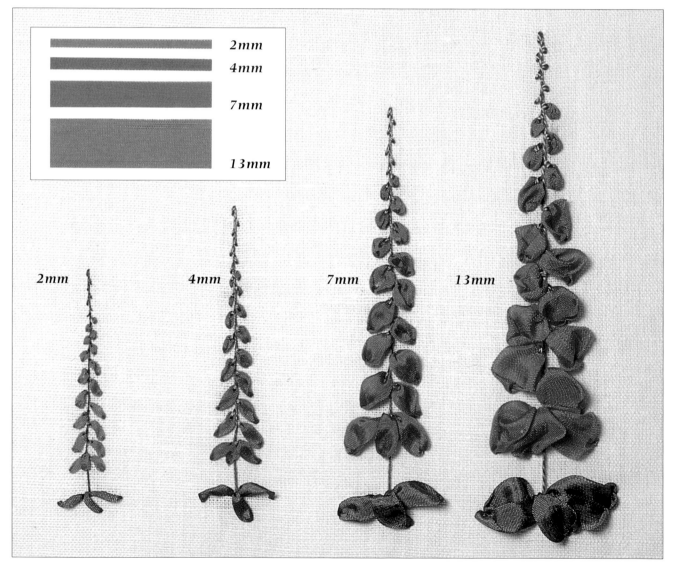

Each of these complete foxglove stems has been worked using exactly the same number of stitches but with a different width of ribbon in each case.

Anchoring ribbons

Narrow ribbon (2 and 4mm wide) can be anchored behind the fabric with a knot. However, wider ribbon makes rather large knots, so I always take one end of ribbon through to the back of the fabric and anchor it with a strand of embroidery thread as shown below. When the ribbon stitches are complete, fasten off all widths of ribbon with a strand of embroidery thread sewn into the back of the last ribbon stitch.

2 and 4mm ribbon

Tie a knot in one end of 2 and 4mm silk ribbon and, using chenille needles Nos. 24 and 18 respectively, take the ribbon through the fabric from the back to the front. Continue from step 3 of the 7 and 13mm ribbon instructions.

7 and 13mm ribbon

1. Cut a length of 7 or 13mm ribbon and thread a short length into a No. 18 chenille needle. Take the short end through to the back of the fabric.

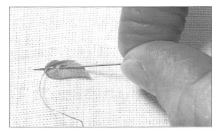

2. Secure the short end with a strand of toning embroidery thread, placing the stitches where they will be concealed behind the first silk ribbon stitch.

3. Now look at where the ribbon comes through to the right side of the fabric. The edges will either curl upwards in a concave shape, or downwards in a convex shape – you cannot control this shape. A convex shape is ideal and you can turn or flatten a concave one (see step 4).

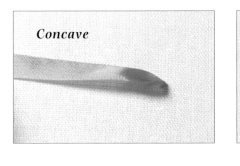

Concave

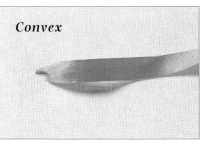

Convex

4. Turn and/or flatten the ribbon using the eye end of a large needle. Hold the ribbon flat on the fabric and gently stroke the needle along the underside of the ribbon.

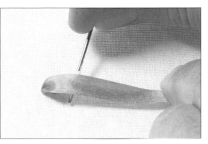

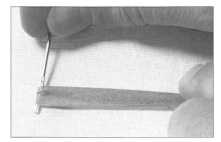

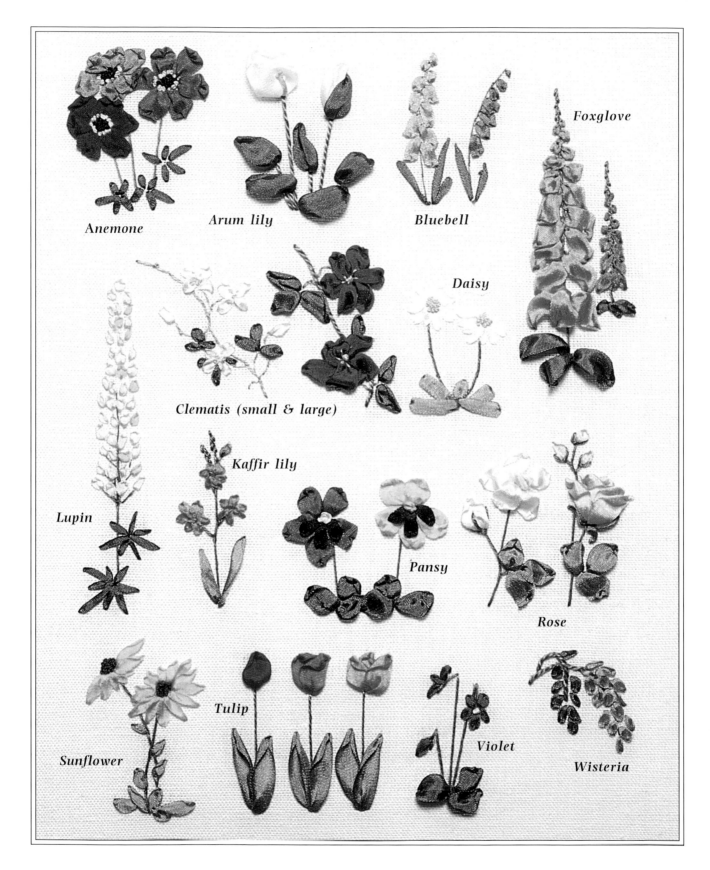

Anemone

Arum lily

Bluebell

Foxglove

Clematis (small & large)

Daisy

Lupin

Kaffir lily

Pansy

Rose

Sunflower

Tulip

Violet

Wisteria

Ribbon stitch

This stitch is unique to ribbon embroidery. Its shape depends on three variables: the size of the initial loop; the needle insertion point across the width of the ribbon; and the tension of the final loop. The flat petals of the anemone and the pointed ones of the foxglove show just how versatile this stitch is.

Centre ribbon stitch

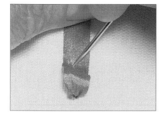

1. Anchor a short end of the ribbon (see page 13), form a small loop, place the point of the needle in the centre of the ribbon then pass it through to the back.

2. At the back of the work, hold the ribbon close to the fabric and gently pull the ribbon through, a short length at a time.

Left ribbon stitch

For this variation, pass the needle through the ribbon at the left selvedge at step 1.

Right ribbon stitch

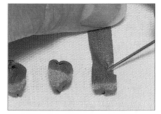

For this variation, pass the needle through the ribbon at the right selvedge at step 1.

3. Pull the ribbon very gently when it is almost through.

4. Stop pulling as soon as the stitch is formed – when the ribbon curls in on itself and just starts to disappear.

Tip: *If a ribbon stitch is pulled too tight, its distinctive shape will be lost. It is also possible to lose a completed stitch when working the next one. To avoid this, place a finger or thumb on the completed stitch. Occasionally, it is possible to ease the ribbon back, but usually mistakes are impossible to correct. The ribbon is damaged when it is stitched through itself, so it is best to cut it away from the fabric and start again.*

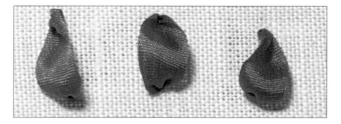

The three stitches: left, centre and right ribbon stitch at twice their actual size.

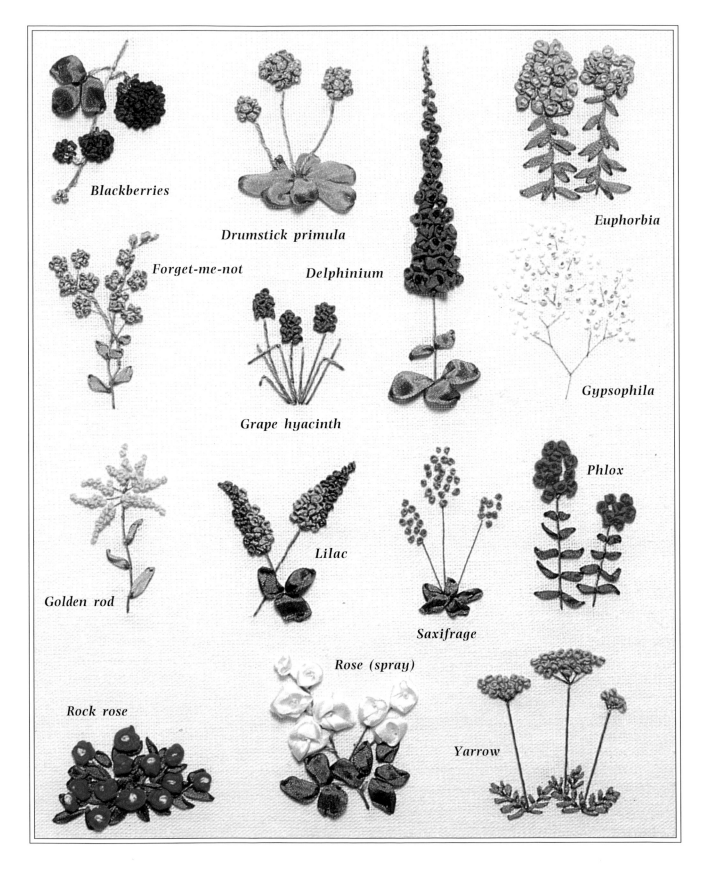

Blackberries

Drumstick primula

Delphinium

Euphorbia

Forget-me-not

Gypsophila

Grape hyacinth

Golden rod

Lilac

Saxifrage

Phlox

Rock rose

Rose (spray)

Yarrow

French knots

The shape of this traditional knot is ideal for creating a wide range of flowers, some of which are shown opposite. The size of the knot depends on the width of ribbon; the number of loops round the needle; and ribbon tension. French knots will add delicacy or weight to a design – from the tiny 2mm ribbon ones for the gypsophila to the 7mm ribbon ones used for the rose spray.

Basic stitch

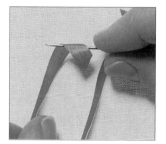 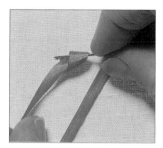  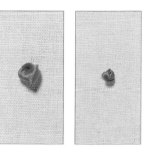

1. Anchor the ribbon (see page 13). Hold the point of a needle behind the ribbon coming up through the fabric, and wrap it once round the needle.

2. Hold the ribbon on the needle and then push the needle back through the fabric close to where the ribbon comes up.

3. Carefully start to pull the ribbon through to the back of the fabric.

4. Stop pulling when the loop in the ribbon disappears into the knot. This will make a loose knot (left). Pull the ribbon tighter to make a small knot (right).

Large stitches

Add a few twists to the ribbon and then wrap the twisted ribbon round the needle two or three times to make a bulkier, more textured knot.

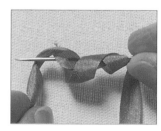

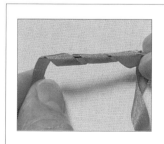

Tip: *Avoid winding the ribbon flat round the needle – when the ribbon is pulled through the fabric, the ribbon will slide inside itself like a telescope and lose its bulk.*

I worked this selection of French knots using 2, 4, 7 and 13mm ribbon (left to right) and one-, two- and three-loops round the needle (top to bottom).

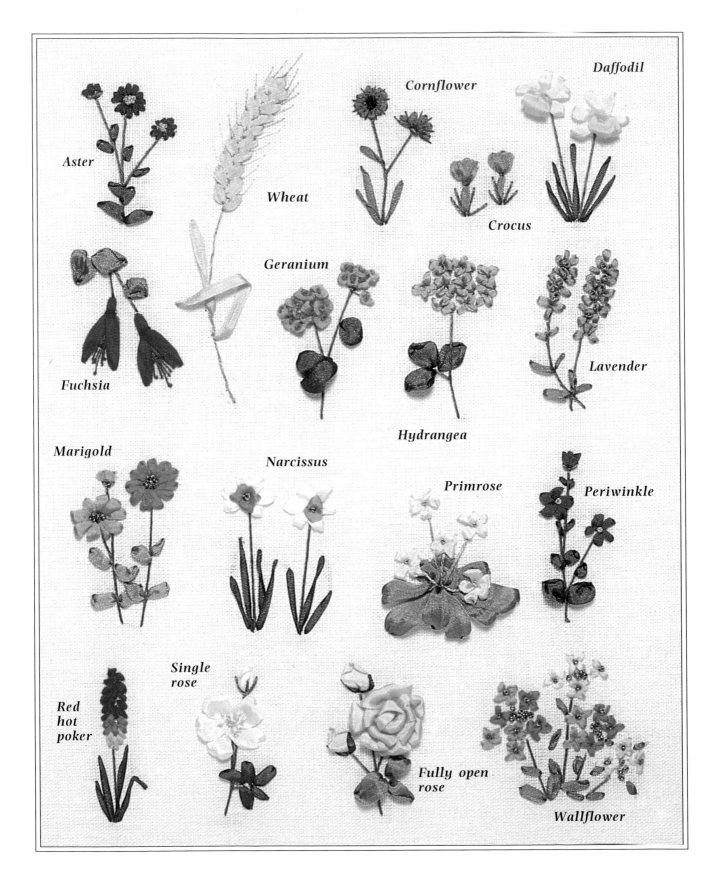

Aster

Wheat

Cornflower

Daffodil

Crocus

Geranium

Fuchsia

Hydrangea

Lavender

Marigold

Narcissus

Primrose

Periwinkle

Red hot poker

Single rose

Fully open rose

Wallflower

Straight stitch

This simple stitch is used in a variety of ways to make all the flowers opposite. The characteristics of the stitch are affected by its length and tension; by the width of the ribbon and any twists that you might add; and by its start and finish positions. For example, the primrose petals are worked by bringing them up at the outer edge and taking them down at the centre, whilst the ribbon is brought up at the centre, then taken down at the edge to create the primrose leaves.

Basic stitch

Anchor the ribbon (see page 13), then take it back down through the fabric, pulling it over the eye of a needle to control the shape. Pull the stitch flat, or allow it to twist or form a loop.

Geranium

Randomly work a cluster of small straight stitch loops with 4mm ribbon. Pull down the centre of each loop with a French knot sewn with one strand of embroidery thread.

Fully open rose

1. Make a two-loop French knot (see page 17) with 7mm ribbon. Work five short straight stitches close to the French knot, making loops the height of the French knot.

2. Work seven more straight stitches round the outside – keep each stitch close to the first circle of petals.

Wheat

Use a fine pencil to mark the centre line of the stem. Work a 4mm centre ribbon stitch (see page 15) for the top grain. Work straight stitches alternating them down each side of the stem – overlap each grain slightly at the stem.

Narcissus

Work six 4mm straight stitch petals from the petal edge to the centre. Work a straight stitch for the trumpet, then pull it down with a French knot sewn with two strands of embroidery thread. Work flat and twisted straight stitches with 2mm ribbon for the leaves.

Tip: *Sometimes, the ribbon becomes twisted as you pull it through the fabric.*

Use the eye end of a needle to flatten a length of ribbon from the centre outwards and bunch the twists at the other end.

Keep tension on the flat part of the ribbon and carefully pull the twisted part through to the back of the fabric.

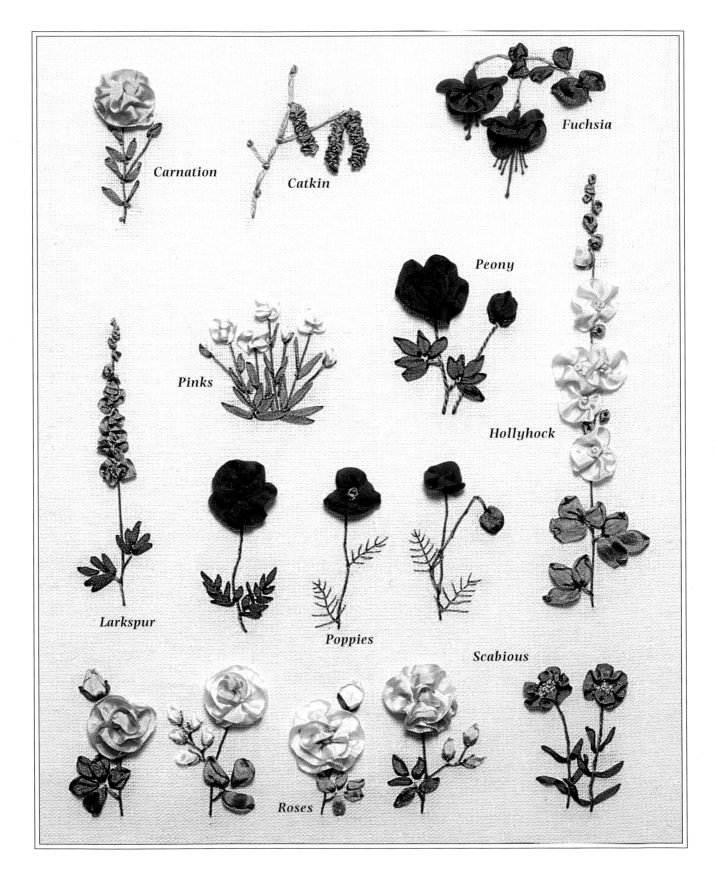

Carnation

Catkin

Fuchsia

Peony

Pinks

Hollyhock

Larkspur

Poppies

Scabious

Roses

Gathering techniques

Silk ribbon gathered with a row of running stitches is used to create a range of flowers, some of which are shown opposite. The effect created depends on the width of ribbon, and the placement and size of the running stitches (see pages 22–23). Tiny stitches give a smooth frill, larger ones a deeper flute. For the purposes of illustration, I have used a contrasting thread rather than a toning one in the photographs below.

Basic method

 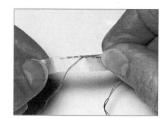  

1. Cut a 20cm length of ribbon. Use a fine needle and a knotted, single strand of embroidery thread to work a tiny stitch over the selvedge 5mm from one end.

2. Work a row of small running stitches very close to one selvedge. Stop 5mm from the other end of the ribbon. Do not cut the thread.

3. Thread the knotted end of the ribbon into a large needle and take it through to the back of the fabric.

4. Use another thread to anchor the knotted end to the fabric (see page 13). Bring this thread back up to the front, close to the ribbon, and place it to one side.

 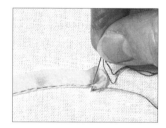  

5. Lightly gather 10mm of ribbon and anchor it close to the mid point of the gather. Bring the anchor thread up to the front.

6. Lightly gather a little more ribbon and anchor this to the fabric so that the ribbon starts to wrap round and form a small circle.

7. Work round and round, gradually increasing the length of the gathers.

8. Continue until only 10mm of gathers are left. Tie off the anchor thread on the back of the fabric. Leave the gathering thread on top.

9. Take the end of the ribbon down through the fabric, leaving the last gathered section and thread at the front. Fasten off the end of the ribbon with the anchoring thread.

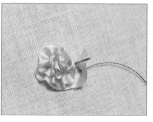

10. Finally, gently tighten the gathering thread and use the fine needle to take the thread down through the fabric. Fasten off at the back of the fabric with a few small stitches.

Variations

Variations of the gathering technique are used to create all the flowers featured on page 20. Some of them have particular characteristics and I have included details of how to place running stitches, and how to work the gathered ribbon, for a few of the more complex flowers.

Catkins I love catkins and I have found this simple way of creating them in silk ribbon. The completed catkins can be attached to the fabric at both ends, or just at the top end and allowed to hang freely.

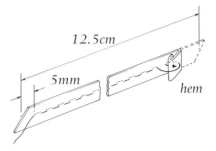

1. Cut a 12.5cm length of 4mm ribbon. Use a single strand of toning thread to make a concealed hem (see diagram). Work a row of small running stitches through the centre as shown.

2. Start to gather the ribbon; ensure that you conceal the hem. Continue gathering the ribbon until it is long enough, then take the ribbon and thread through to the back of the fabric. Use the thread to anchor the ribbon.

Fuchsia I use this technique for a fully open fuchsia where the skirt (or corolla) is clearly visible. Other fuchsia flower heads can be created with different types of stitch.

1. Cut a 7.5cm length of 7mm ribbon; for this design, cut opposite angles at each end. Work a row of running stitches as shown. Note the two offset stitches – these create a staggered gather.

2. Thread both ribbon ends in a needle, take them to the back of the fabric but leave the gathering thread on top. Part the two ends of the ribbon and anchor them separately with another thread; bring this anchor thread to the front.

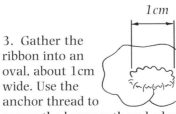

3. Gather the ribbon into an oval, about 1cm wide. Use the anchor thread to secure the lower gathered edge with a few small stitches. Fasten off at the back of the fabric.

4. Fold the top half of the oval shape down and secure the gathered edge in place with the gathering thread. Fasten off on the back of the fabric.

Two-tone roses Many roses have shaded petals and you can recreate this effect by using two shades of ribbon sewn together and gathered as one. Use either two lengths of the same width of ribbon or two lengths of different widths.

Cut two 18cm lengths of two shades of 7mm ribbon. Lay the light shade of ribbon over the dark one so that a dark edge shows at the top . Work a row of running stitches through both ribbons along the lower edges. Build up the flower as shown on page 21 – this arrangement gives a two-tone rose with the darker shade of colour at the back of the flower.

Two-tone rose made with 7mm ribbon.

Two-tone rose made with 4mm and 7mm ribbon.

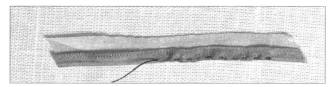

If you use different width ribbons, arrange them so that they align along one edge then work a row of running stitches along this edge.

Larkspur Small ribbon rosettes are built up along a coton à broder stem (see page 28). Work a row of running stitches, close to the selvedge, but only half way along a 25cm length of 4mm ribbon.

Take the knotted end of the ribbon through to the back of the fabric, about 2.5cm up the stem, and anchor it. Thread the other end of the ribbon in a needle. Gather a short length of ribbon into a small rosette and then take the ribbon through to the back leaving the rosette at the front. Bring the ribbon back to the front and make a slightly smaller rosette. Continue working up the stem, stopping just below the top. Finish the flower by working a few tiny straight stitch buds.

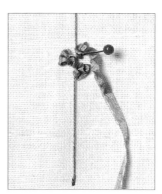

Tips Use a gathering thread that tones with the ribbon, and an anchor thread that tones with the fabric.

Cut gathering thread two to three times the length of the ribbon to be gathered.

Lazy daisy stitch

This traditional stitch is also known as detached chain stitch. It is very useful and easy to work. The stitch can be altered simply by varying the size of the stitch, and by using different widths of ribbon. For example, compare the tiny stitches made with 2mm ribbon in the pussy willow, to those made with 4mm ribbon forming the iris, or the bulkier twisted stitches used to create the rose.

Basic stitch

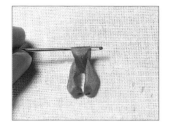

1. Anchor one end of the ribbon on the back of the fabric (see page 13), then take the other end back down just to the right.

2. Carefully pull the ribbon to leave a loop at the front. Use a needle to ease away any twists as shown on page 19.

3. Hold the loop down with your thumb and bring the ribbon up just inside the top of the loop. Use a needle to prevent twisting and take the ribbon over the loop and back through the fabric to form a closing loop.

Enlarged view of the finished lazy daisy stitch.

Variations

Work a chain of lazy daisy stitches (right) by repeating steps 1 and 2, starting each successive stitch inside the top of the previous loop. Finish the top of the chain with a closing loop as shown in step 3.

Form a twisted chain (far right) in a similar way but add a twist to the loop form in step 2.

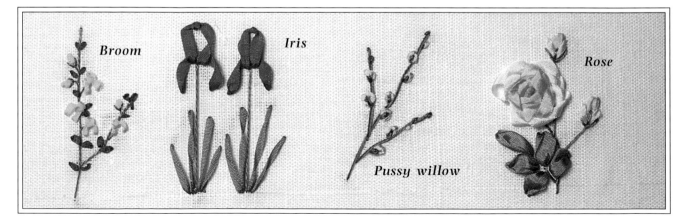

Broom

Iris

Rose

Pussy willow

Bows

A silk ribbon bow will add a touch of luxury to any piece of embroidery.
Bows are quick to work and look effective in any size ribbon. The bows
shown here are made with 0.5m of 7mm ribbon.

Draw a short horizontal guide line where the central knot of the bow will lay. Work a loop of ribbon at the left-hand side of the knot position, using a lazy daisy or straight stitch. Make another similar loop on the right-hand side. For a double straight stitch bow, work the second loops inside the first ones. Work two straight stitch streamers; bring the ribbon up at the knot position and down at the end of the streamer. Make

one streamer longer than the other. Finally, work a straight stitch knot bringing the ribbon up through the fabric above the left-hand side of the guide line and take it down below the right-hand side of the line.

To make the looped bow (right) embroider a single straight stitch loop at the centre of the bow and then work nine more loops round the outside but close to the centre point. Work two streamers as above.

Lazy daisy stitch

Double straight stitch

Single straight stitch

Straight stitch loops

Using threads

A selection of threads is useful for stems. Vary their colour, thickness,
and texture for each different flower – this will add realism to your
work. A mixture of different threads can be used to great effect.

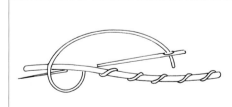

Couching *A single strand of toning thread is used to secure another thread in place. This is useful when working curved stems.*

Fly stitch *This is a single open looped stitch similar to a lazy daisy stitch. It is often worked as a calyx for flowers such as rose buds.*

Pistil stitch *This stitch is useful for stamens. The thread is brought up to the front of the fabric, wrapped round a needle a few times and then taken back down, a short distance away.*

Spring flowers

This design, with its foxgloves, irises and primroses, is embroidered on linen/cotton evenweave and is a good first project to introduce the four basic stitches. I have listed the total lengths and colours of the ribbons and threads that I used to make the picture below, but you could use your own colour scheme.

The template given opposite is used to define the basic structure of the plants and their position relative to each other. The silk ribbon flowers and leaves are then added as necessary to build up the distinctive shape of each plant. The other templates given in this book follow the same pattern.

RIBBONS

Foxglove flowers
(1 & 2) – 2m of 7mm deep pink (No. 128)
(3 & 4) – 2m of 7mm dusky pink (No. 163)
(5) – 0.5m of 4mm deep pink (No. 128)

Foxglove leaves
(1, 2 & 3) – 1m of 7mm green (No. 21)
(4 & 5) – 0.5m of 4mm green (No. 21)

Iris flowers
(1 & 2) – 0.5m of 4mm light mauve (No. 178)
(3, 4 & 5) – 0.5m of 4mm deep mauve (No. 179)

Iris leaves
1m of 2mm soft green (No. 33)

Primrose flowers
1.5m of 4mm pale yellow (No. 13)

Primrose leaves
1.5m of 7mm moss green (No. 20)

FABRIC

Linen/cotton evenweave 25 x 30cm

THREADS

Pale khaki and toning stranded embroidery threads

Coton à broder and pearl cotton threads in shades of green for flower stems.

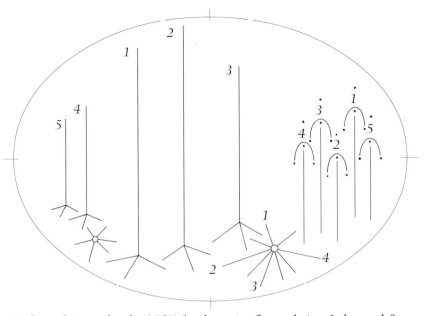

Enlarge this template by 165% for the spring flower design. I always define a border round a design and I include quarter marks on circular and oval shapes – these are used when repositioning the template during the progress of the embroidery. The numbers shown against the different sets of plants indicate the order in which they are worked. They are also referred to in the list of ribbons.

Transferring the design

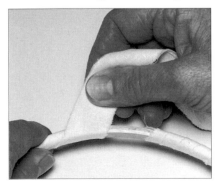

1. Bind the inner frame with 2.5cm wide strips of cotton. Overlap the end and secure with a few small stitches.

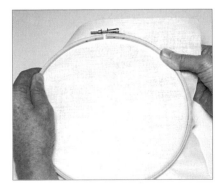

2. Place the fabric over the bound inner frame, position the outer frame on top and press down firmly to stretch the fabric. Tighten the frame.

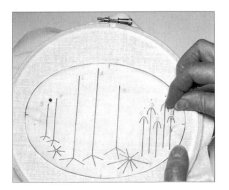

3. Photocopy the template, then cut round the oval border and place the template on the fabric. Line up the foxglove stems with the grain of the fabric and secure with two dressmaker's pins.

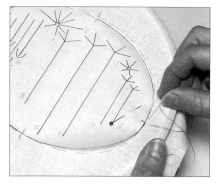

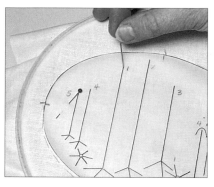

4. Tack round the outside of the template, adding a single stitch at right angles for each quarter mark. These quarter marks will enable you to reposition the template as necessary.

5. Push a large needle through the template and fabric at the top and bottom of the stem of foxglove No. 1. Mark the fabric through the holes with a fine pencil. Remove the template.

Working the foxglove stems

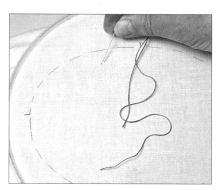

1. Hold a length of thread between the two dots to check that the stem lays with the grain of the fabric. Adjust the bottom position of the stem as required.

2. Bring a knotted length of green coton à broder up through the fabric at the bottom of stem No. 1, and then back down at the top.

3. Bring the thread up through the fabric outside the template area. Place the needle in the fabric and, keeping the thread taut, wind it round the needle to anchor it.

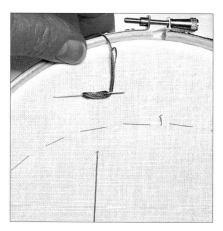

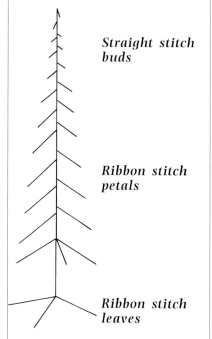

Straight stitch buds

Ribbon stitch petals

Ribbon stitch leaves

I have included this diagram to show you how I work the petals and leaves of a foxglove. I start with the lowest petals and work in ribbon stitch up the stem, allowing the petals to overlap slightly and to make each successive stitch slightly shorter and tighter. I finish with a few small straight stitches, some with ribbon and then a few with thread.

Embroidering the foxglove

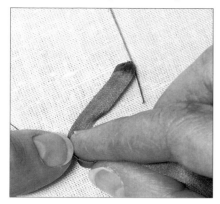

1. Thread a No. 18 chenille needle with 7mm pink ribbon. Refer to the stitch diagram opposite, take a short end of the ribbon down through the fabric, close to the stem. Anchor the short end as explained on page 13.

2. Use centre ribbon stitch to work the bottom three petals. Continue up the stem with more centre ribbon stitches, alternating them either side of the stem. Make each new stitch a little smaller than the previous one. Stop 2.5cm from the top of the stem.

3. Now, work a few buds in straight stitch. Bring the ribbon up slightly away from the stem (this will be the tip of the bud) and take it down close to the stem. Make each new stitch smaller and tighter than the previous one. Stop about 5mm from the top.

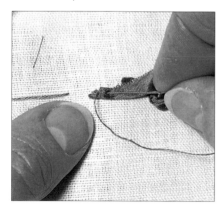

4. Anchor the ribbon at the back of the fabric with a single strand of toning thread; sew into the back of the straight stitches just worked. Cut off any excess ribbon.

5. Release the green stem thread from its temporary anchor point and pull it through to the back of the fabric. Rethread it and bring it up to the front, slightly below the top of the stem, on the same side as the last pink bud.

6. Keep the stem thread taut and then take the thread down through the tip of the stem to form a tiny unopened bud.

7. Work a second green bud the other side of the stem, just above the top pink bud. Use the same thread and straight stitch to work a calyx and so attach each flower to the stem. To do this, bring the thread up through the top of each flower and take it down either through or close to, but not over, the stem. Do not add calyxes to the three petals at the bottom set.

8. Bring the thread up through the fabric at the base of the stem and fasten off with a couple of stitches. These stitches will be concealed when the leaves are worked.

9. Take a short end of a length of 7mm green ribbon through the fabric at the base of the stem and anchor it. Use centre ribbon stitch to embroider three leaves as shown on the template (see page 26). Replace the template, using the quarter marks as a guide, and repeat the procedure to create the rest of the foxgloves.

Embroidering the irises

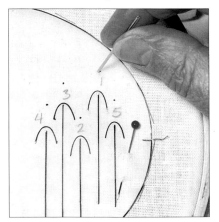

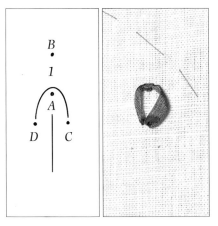

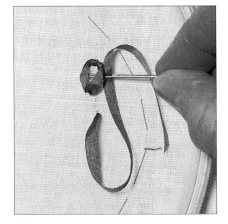

1. Replace the template and use a needle and a fine pencil to mark the top and bottom of the stem of iris No. 1. Refer to the diagram (right) and mark points A–D of the flower head in a similar manner.

2. Use a length of 4mm light mauve ribbon to embroider a lazy daisy stitch as shown on page 24. Anchor a short end through point A and form the closing loop at point B.

3. Bring the ribbon up through point C and, using the eye of the needle to avoid snagging, take the ribbon behind the lazy daisy stitch.

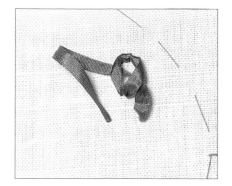

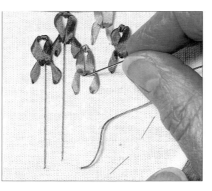

4. Take the ribbon back down at point D. Allow a slight twist but avoid pulling the ribbon too tight. Anchor the ribbon at the back of the fabric. Repeat steps 2–4 to create the other iris flower heads.

5. Work the stems with a length of green coton à broder. Start at the left-hand side and work across the design, bringing the thread up at the base of the stem and down close to each flower head.

6. Anchor a length of 2mm soft green ribbon through the base of the left-hand stem (see page 13) and work some leaves in straight stitch. Make each leaf a different length and allow the ribbon to twist once or twice. Work across the design, adding leaves to the base of each stem.

Embroidering the primroses

1. Replace the template, mark the centre of the primroses and the ends of the longest leaves. Use 7mm moss green ribbon to work straight stitch leaves. Bring the ribbon up through the centre and back down at the outer edge of each leaf. Use a needle to help keep the ribbon flat (see also page 19). Fill in the gaps with smaller leaves.

2. Use 4mm pale yellow ribbon and straight stitch to embroider five evenly spaced petals for each flower head. Bring the ribbon up at the petal edge and take it down at the centre.

3. Use one strand of pale khaki embroidery thread to make a one-loop French knot in the centre of each flower. Use the same thread and straight stitch to make the flower stems; work these behind the flowers as necessary.

Bouquet of roses

This beautiful bouquet of roses is embroidered on silk dupion and tied with a silk ribbon bow to add a final touch of luxury. The fully open flowers are worked in straight stitch around a French knot; and I have made them look different by shading some of them and angling others forward by omitting some of the outer petals. The half open roses, the buds and the leaves are all worked in variations of ribbon stitch.

RIBBONS

Flower heads

2.5m of 7mm deep salmon (No. 112)

2m of 7mm apricot (No. 167)

2m of 7mm cream (No. 156)

Leaves

1m of 7mm moss green (No. 20)

1m of 7mm deep moss green (No. 72)

Calyx for half-open flowers

0.5m of 2mm khaki (No. 56)

Bow

0.5m of 7mm cream (No. 156)

FABRIC

Pale cream silk dupion 30cm square

THREADS

Green coton à broder for stems

Selection of toning stranded embroidery threads

Refer to the step-by-step instructions for the colours used to make the flower heads and buds. Each of the fully open roses will need approximately 40cm of ribbon.

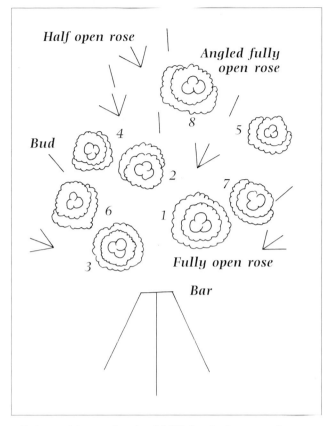

Enlarge this template by 150% for the bouquet of roses. The numbers on this template are used to identify similar roses and are referred to in the step-by-step instructions. Tack the border on to the fabric as shown on page 28.

Making a fully open rose

1. Use the template to mark the centre of each full rose with a pencil (see page 28). Anchor a length of 7mm deep salmon ribbon beneath the centre of rose No. 1 and embroider a loose, three-loop French knot (see page 17).

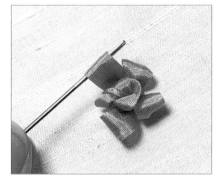

2. Work five straight stitch loops as petals around the French knot; keep the ribbon at flat as possible using the eye end of a large needle (see page 19).

3. Make seven more straight stitch loops round the outside of the first row. Work each of these under the first row of petals, as close as possible to the centre.

Two-tone rose

Rose No. 3 is a two-tone version of the fully open rose (see page 33). Work steps 1 and 2 with deep salmon ribbon and work step 3 with apricot ribbon.

Angled rose

Roses Nos. 2 and 4–8 are two-toned angled flowers. These are worked as the other fully open roses (see page 33) except that in step 3, two or three petals are omitted. Deep salmon is used for rose 2, deep salmon and apricot ribbons for roses 4 and 5, and apricot and cream for the rest.

Half open rose

1. Reposition the template and mark the positions of the base and petal tips of each half-open rose. Use cream ribbon and work a centre ribbon stitch for the first petal (see page 15), from the base out to the tip.

2. Bring the ribbon back up at the base, and work a left-hand ribbon stitch to the left of the first petal and a right-hand one to the right of the first petal. Fasten off. Repeat steps 1 and 2 for the other half-open flowers (see template).

Buds

Reposition the template and mark the top and bottom of each bud. Use very short lengths of deep salmon ribbon to work single centre ribbon stitches for each bud. Fasten off the ribbon after each bud has been worked.

Stems and calixes

1. Replace the template and mark the position of the bar and lower stems. Keep the fabric taut and use a length of green coton à broder to work a straight stitch across the bar. Work the lower stems; always bring the needle up through the fabric at the bar and back down at the base of the stem. Work the middle stem first, then the outer two stems and, finally, work stems of different lengths in between. Work straight stitch stems above the bar, bringing the thread up at the bar and taking it down tight against each flower head. Work the full and half-open roses first, taking the thread behind flowers as necessary.

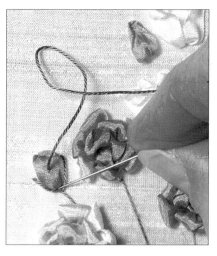

2. Work stems for the buds, then add a calyx; work a fly stitch either side of the bud (see page 25) and a straight stitch in the middle.

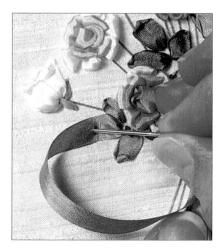

3. Now change to 2mm khaki ribbon and work a calyx on each half-open rose, using one left ribbon stitch and one right ribbon stitch.

4. Change to 7mm ribbon and use moss and deep moss green ribbon and centre ribbon stitch to work the leaves at random. Use the darker shade for those at the base of the bouquet.

5. Work a double straight stitch bow (see page 25) to complete the bouquet.

Country garden

French knots and 4mm ribbon are used in abundance in this design of delphiniums and yarrow. Vary the size and tension of each French knot to create shape and texture. The daisies are worked in ribbon stitch with French knot centres in much the same way as the primroses on page 31.

RIBBONS

Delphinium flowers

(1, 2 & 3) – 4m of 4mm deep blue (No. 46)

(4, 5, 7 & 8) – 5m of 4mm mid blue (No. 126)

(6) – 1.5m of 4mm pale blue (No. 44)

Delphinium leaves

1.5m of 7mm deep green (No. 21)

0.5m of 2mm deep green (No. 21)

Yarrow flowers

3m of 4mm gold (No. 54)

1m of 4mm yellow (No. 15)

Yarrow leaves

1m of 2mm soft green (No. 33)

Daisy flower heads

4m of 2mm white (No. 3)

Daisy leaves

1m of 4mm moss green No. 20)

FABRIC

Cream surface linen 25 x 30cm

THREADS

Coton à broder in shades of green for the stems of the delphiniums and daisies.

Two or three different shades of blue stranded embroidery thread for the centres of the delphiniums

Pale khaki stranded embroidery thread for the yarrow stems

Selection of toning stranded embroidery threads

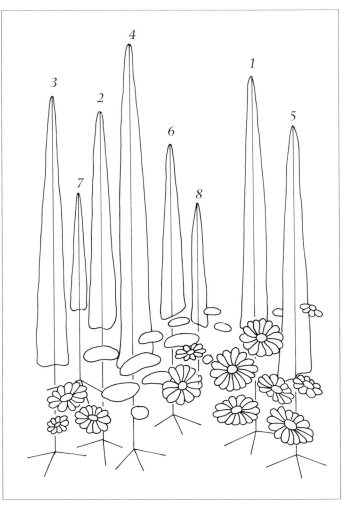

Enlarge this template by 140%. Tack the border on to the fabric (see page 28) and then work the stems of the delphiniums in a similar way as the foxglove stems on page 28, but from the top of the stem down to the base.

Delphiniums

Start embroidering the delphiniums about a quarter of the way up the stem. Work five or six quite loose, three-loop French knots (see page 17) up either side and over the stem. Now work some smaller, two-loop French knots randomly on either side of the larger ones. Leave space between some of the flowers. Finally make some one-loop French knots on each side to give shape and depth. Continue up the stem, gradually making the knots smaller and tighter to form a tapered column. Work a few tiny straight stitch buds at the top. Re-tension the stem and fasten it off at the base (see page 29).

Yarrow

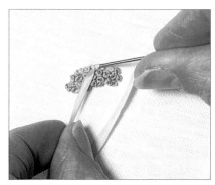

Build up the bulk of the yarrow flower heads with 4mm gold ribbon. Work two-loop and one-loop French knots to create form and texture. Create highlights with a few one-loop French knots worked with 4mm yellow ribbon.

The finished embroidery.

Complete the delphiniums with three ribbon stitch leaves worked with deep green 7mm ribbon. Add a few leaves up the stem with 2mm ribbon.

Work straight stitch stems for the yarrow with coton à broder and then use 2mm green ribbon to work the fly stitch leaves.

Work the daisies using 2mm white ribbon and ribbon stitch. Combine one strand of cream and pale green embroidery thread to work one-loop French knots for the centres. Use straight stitch and 4mm moss green ribbon for the leaves.

Poppies and wheat

I have used a black surface linen background in this picture to accentuate the simplicity of the design of wild poppies and wheat. A variation of the gathering technique is used to create the poppies, whilst the wheat is embroidered with straight stitch as shown on page 19.

Full size template. Stitch a border on to the fabric and then mark the centre of the poppy flower heads with a pencil as shown on page 28.

RIBBONS

Poppies

1m of 7mm red (No. 2)
0.5m of 4mm khaki (No. 56)
3m of 4mm corn (No. 35)
3m of 2mm deep green (No. 21)
0.5m of 7mm deep green (No. 21)

FABRIC

Black surface linen 25 x 30cm

THREADS

Coton à broder in shades of green
Selection of toning stranded embroidery threads

OTHER ITEMS

Pale colour transfer pencil

Note

In the step-by-step instructions, a contrasting thread has been used for the gathering thread to allow the stitches to be clearly visible. Normally, you would use a toning thread.

Also for the purposes of clarity, pins have been used to hold the ribbon in position. Pins will damage the ribbon so, in practice, hold the ribbon down with a finger or thumb.

5cm 6.5cm

1. Cut a 12.5cm length of 7mm red ribbon and work a row of gathering stitches (using a toning shade of thread) as shown above, leaving 5mm of free ribbon at each end. Do not cut off the excess thread.

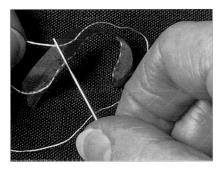

2. Anchor the knotted end of the ribbon at the back of the fabric with a length of black thread. Bring the thread to the front. Gather 6cm of ribbon (up to the crossover point) and shape the frill as a small horseshoe; place the chenille needle into the fabric 4mm to one side of the start point. For clarity, I have used dressmaker's pins to hold the frill in position.

3. Make a loop in the gathering thread and pass both it and the free end of the ribbon through the eye of the needle.

4. Carefully pull the ribbon through the fabric until the crossover stitches in the middle disappear. On the back of the fabric, pull the gathering thread out of the eye of the needle then remove the end of the ribbon.

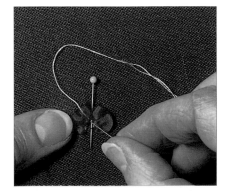

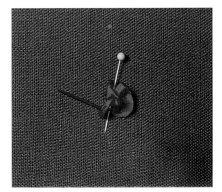

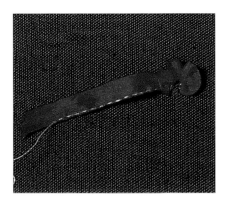

5. Return to the front of the work and, keeping the gathers even, use the anchor thread to secure the gathered selvedge with a few tiny stitches. Take care not to catch the ribbon at the back.

6. Rethread the ribbon and gathering thread on the needle. Fold back the left-hand side of the horseshoe and bring the needle through to the front, close to the folded-back frill.

7. Carefully pull the ribbon and gathering thread through to the front. Adjust the ribbon so that the gathering stitches are at the bottom.

8. Thread the free end of the ribbon into the needle and take it through to the back, just behind the right-hand side of the frill. Leave the gathering thread at the front. Secure the end of the ribbon with the anchor thread, then cut off the excess thread.

9. Hold the frill flat and carefully pull the gathering thread to create the bottom petal of the flower. Secure the gathered selvedge with the gathering thread; work it in a straight line across the horseshoe shape of the top petal. Fasten off. Work the petals of the other poppies in a similar manner.

The finished embroidery.

Use 4mm khaki ribbon to make a one-loop French knot in the centre of each poppy (see page 17). Use six strands of black embroidery thread to work three French knots close round the centre knot. Embroider the buds in the same way as the primrose leaves on page 31. Lay in stems of green coton à broder, curving them to the template, and couch them in place with a single thread of stranded cotton (see page 25). Use 2mm ribbon to work the leaves in a combination of fly stitch and straight stitch.

Embroider the ears of wheat as shown on page 19. Use single straight stitches for the wheat leaves, folding them in behind the stems as necessary.

Blackberries

Silk ribbon French knots in deep purple make the blackberries look plump, shiny and ready to eat. To create the rounded effect of each berry, the tension is varied as the one- and two-loop French knots are worked (see page 17).

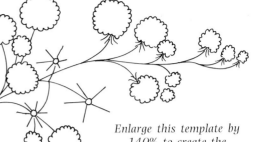

Enlarge this template by 140% to create the blackberries design.

RIBBONS

Berries

3m of 4mm deep purple (No. 86)

1m of 4mm red (No. 50)

0.5m of 2mm soft green (No. 33)

Flowers

1m of 7mm just pink (No. 5)

Leaves

1m of 7mm deep moss (No. 72)

FABRIC

Linen/cotton evenweave 20 x 25cm

THREADS

Selection of toning stranded embroidery threads

1. Use purple ribbon to work three, fairly loose, two-loop French knots close together for the centre of a berry. Surround these with one-loop French knots; make them tighter and smaller towards the edge.

2. Change to red ribbon and work a few one-loop French knots at random into any tiny space to create blemishes on the berry.

3. Now use 2mm soft green ribbon to work a few small straight stitches for the calyx on some of the berries.

The finished embroidery.

Add some unripe berries using one-loop French knots worked with six strands of embroidery thread. Use six strands of thread for the main stem; divide them off to two strands for the last three berries. Couch the stem in place with a single strand. Work the flowers with pink ribbon and straight stitch; use one strand of thread and one-loop French knots for the stamens. Work the leaves randomly, using ribbon stitch and 7mm green ribbon.

Stencilling a background

Stencilling is a very effective way of creating a background for three-dimensional embroidery. Dry stencil paints and brushes are readily available and they are easy to use. Keep the shapes simple and pay special attention to light and shade – these points will add realism to the finished piece.

In this project, I show you how to stencil two very simple plant pots. I have filled mine with a fuchsia and a geranium, but you could choose different flowers to put in yours.

Full size template for the flower pots

I chose to embroider a standard fuchsia and a geranium in these stencilled flower pots.

The thick stem of the fuchsia is a mixture of different shades of stranded embroidery threads. Straight stitch and 4mm ribbon is used to create the flowers, and 4mm ribbon and ribbon stitch form the leaves.

Two shades of pink 4mm ribbon are used for the geraniums. Each petal is a straight stitch loop into which is added a one-loop French knot, sewn with two strands of embroidery thread. The leaves are very full straight stitches.

1. Trace the flower pots on to a stiff piece of card and cut them out with a craft knife.

2. Place the stencil on the fabric and hold in position. Pick up a small amount of brown dry stencil paint on a stencil brush. Remove excess paint on a piece of scrap fabric and then gently brush the paint on to the embroidery fabric. Work round the edges of the stencil to define the flower pot shapes.

3. Add a little more colour to the brush and work it into the pots to create shaded areas; remember to leave highlights. Pick up some of the same colour with the tip of a cocktail stick and carefully draw in the rim of the pot.

4. Create shadow on the ground below the pots. Do not pick up any more colour; just use the paint that is still on the brush. Lightly sweep the brush across the fabric towards, but not into, the stencilled pots.

5. Pick up some green paint on the brush, remove excess paint and then brush this into the shadows to add tone.

Painting a background

Fabric paints can be used to good effect to create lots of depth in an embroidery. In this project I show you how to use just two colours – blue and yellow– to paint a background that will help create a striking floral display.

The pot is first stencilled on to a silk noile background as shown on page 42. Silk noile is used for the background fabric as its rough texture helps create the effect of heavy pottery.

Full size template

1. Place small amounts of blue and yellow fabric paint on a tile palette. Mix these colours together to create light, medium and dark shades of green.

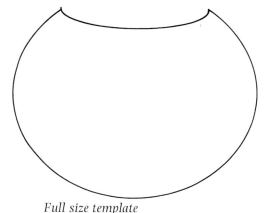

2. Paint soft, sweeping strokes of light green over the background to suggest flower stems.

3. Use medium green to add darker tones.

4. Finally, add dark green to the shaded central area of the background and over the top of the pot. Allow the paints to dry before starting to embroider.

I chose bright yellow roses as the main focus of this display, and these are worked in 7mm ribbon. Long straight stitches of coton à broder are added to give height, then a variety of flowers are embroidered. Different shades and widths of green ribbon are used for the leaves, and these are tucked in behind the flowers. Stems are added randomly to a few of the flowers.

Mounting and framing

When your embroidery is finished, remove the tacked border and tidy up all the loose ends at the back of your work. Take it off the embroidery hoop or frame and lightly press the fabric with an iron, taking care to avoid the embroidered ribbons. Your work is now ready to be framed – you could take it along to your local picture framer, or you could do it yourself.

Framing an embroidery is not difficult. You will need to buy a frame and a mount that complements your work. The mount must fit in the frame and its opening should be sized to give a reasonable amount of space around the embroidery. You will also need a baseboard that is slightly smaller than the mount and which is white on one side, some hardboard, some gummed paper tape, two screw eyes and some cord.

If you want to glaze the embroidery, you will need a sheet of 2mm picture glass and some thin strips of balsa wood or foamboard to lift the mount and the glass away from the top of the ribbon embroidery

1. Apply strips of double-sided tape to all four edges on the coloured side of the baseboard.

2. Position the mount centrally over the embroidery.

3. Carefully place the mount and embroidery on the white side of the baseboard. Check the corners of the baseboard are square to the mount.

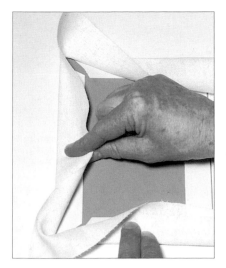

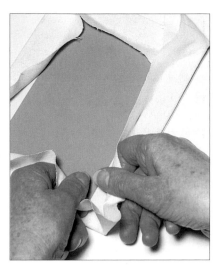

4. Remove the mount and carefully turn the embroidery and baseboard over on to a clean flat surface. Remove the backing from the strips of tape on the two short sides. Hold everything down firmly with one hand, pull one of the short sides of the fabric taut and press the middle of it on to the tape. Stick down the middle of the other short side. Fix the long sides in the same way.

5. Stretch adjacent sides of fabric towards one of the corners and the middle of the baseboard at the same time. Press the fabric down on to the sticky tape, leaving triangular flaps. Stretch and secure the other three corners.

6. Check that the fabric is stretched flat on the right side and re-stretch it if necessary. Fold the corners into a mitre and press them flat with the tip of an iron.

7. Place the frame face down on a flat surface then insert the mount, the embroidery and finally the hardboard. Use strips of gummed paper tape to secure the hardboard to the back of the frame. Insert screw eyes one third of the way down from the top of the frame and tie a cord between them.

If you wish to glaze an embroidery, use double-sided sticky tape to fix strips of balsa wood or foamboard to the back of the mount.

Index